Sowing, reaping, tilling, fallow.

In 2013 I learnt about a plant with a name that startled me. It was a polyantha rose, small, with pink blooms. Its common name—the name it had been registered and sold under—was 'Verdun'. It had been bred in 1918 by a heritage rose nursery in northern France, the Barbier Frères & Compagnie. They launched the Rosa polyantha 'Verdun' in commemoration of the WWI battle that had taken place just two years prior, the so-called 'Hell of Verdun' which had seen the deaths of some 300.000 German and French soldiers. I was curious about this pretty garden rose that had been burdened with commemorating such carnage.

I visited Verdun to meet with a family who were involved in ensuring the continued propagation and circulation of the rose, nearly 100 years after its creation. I explored the site of the former battlefield. The war left these soils so churned with death, mortar shells and toxins that soon after the armistice a state decision was made to plant the spoilt ground with a forest, which was then managed to accelerate its growth. By the time I visited it had the characteristics of a forest three times its actual age. I understood that both the Verdun rose and this planted battlefield forest were playing a specific botanical role in forming how this battle was and is remembered, forgotten and historicised. These plants were being used to garden grief, to garden a national post-war narrative: to garden history.

Rosa Floribunda 'Verdun', 2014

I was gifted a Rosa polyantha 'Verdun' by my new friends. I took it back to Berlin, where, soon after, I accidentally killed it by overwatering it. My care for Verdun was all wrong, and the rose and its name were put in the compost. I began trawling nursery catalogues, horticultural registries and botanical garden inventories, searching for other plants with common names referencing warfare and the military. Alongside the more innocently named 'Morning Dew' and 'Christmas Spirit', I discovered others plants titled Rosa 'Battle of Britain', Clematis 'Heroes of Warsaw', and Daffodil 'Desert Storm'. I began gathering these plants alongside a (generously supplied) replacement Verdun rose. I needed a place to grow my expanding collection, and this led me to a plot in the community gardens of the Tempelhofer Feld, a vast public park which was a former military and civilian tilling airport, Prussian parade ground, Gestapo prison camp (northern edge), and the site of the famous air aid drop in divided Berlin. It's a site which, significantly, has slipped between civilian and military use for decades, if not centuries. The community gardeners joked that if, whilst digging into the soils, I were to hit something metallic, I should quickly bury it and dig my garden further away.

Tempelhofer Feld, summer 2015

Tempelhofer Feld, spring 2021

The stories of those who have bred these plants, and the reasons for their names, are very varied. A nurseryman names his new clematis variety in memory of his son who died in WWI. A Soviet-era Belarusian Botanical Institute honours, with their prize-winning lilac, the female partisans who fought during WWII. Some plant names reflect the politics of the breeder, but many are named as a marketing strategy. For example, following WWI, there are cases of plants being named after battles in the hope that they might appeal to bereaved families, or purchased en masse to be planted in vast state war cemeteries. Some unspectacular cultivars may get a sales boost due to a socially resonant market name, hitching a ride on public sentiment. By the same token, the names of certain minor military men may linger on in gardens and nurseries because of the scent or vivid colour of a rose.

Kunsthalle Osnabrück, spring 2022

The truth behind the naming of certain plants is not always apparent. Was this plant registered 'Memory of Malmedy' intended as a memorial for the infamous massacre that took place in Belgium, or was the breeder commemorating personal peaceful memories of the same place? When the breeder of a bright yellow echinacea flower named their new creation 'Grenade', were they thinking of the imagined aesthetics of the exploding weapon? Or the explosion of seeds the flower casts off into the wind in spring? Or the fruit after which the weapon was named in the 1500s? The language of destruction and rejuvenation blurs. The same goes for the language of garden care itself: to 'strike', 'defend', 'plough', 'compost', 'till', 'sow', 'reap', and 'prune'. 'Trenches' are dug. Species are 'invasive'. We 'defend' saplings against pests and 'force' growth from them in greenhouses.

Over the years, I documented the garden: sketching new growth, painting still lives of its fruit, gathering countless boxes of thorns and deadheaded flowers. However, this extracted ephemera was less exciting to me than the slow tension that emerged through the ongoing process of upkeep that was taking place in the garden itself – the care and control of tending to these plants, and to the language and history they carried with them. How does one tend to a plant which glorifies war? Or one which plays a minor role in nationalist propaganda, or is laden with personal grief? How to take care of that which we would prefer to bury? There is no final answer to this, no still life, just the continuum of season after season.

Kunsthalle Osnabrück, autumn 2022

My father is an avid gardener, and for all my life I have witnessed him gardening like a soldier. He emerges from the greenery covered in scratches, bites and bruises, bandages himself up and heads back out again. He is at war with the plants but he cares for them and the garden is a place of life and vibrant tranquility. My gardening practice on the Tempelhofer Feld is likewise laden with both tenderness and violence: weeding out living beings to allow selected plants to flourish, sawing limbs off of rose bushes to enable airflow, pricking out sprouts and squashing pests. The garden leaves me burning from stinging nettles, torn by thorns. My father's garden is in (so named) Australia, Cammeraygal Land, on soils where frontier wars were fought, wars that, at least when I was growing up there, were not signposted with memorial plaques, were not legible (to me) within the greenery. I wonder if the land, and its battlefields, have been gardened in a way that the Colony may forget this history. Perhaps I am intrigued by the battle-named plants because they carry history of violence in a way that is legible for me in an obvious way—the past emblazoned upon official botanical labels. Grown together, these plants create a history book—a flawed and limited and messy anthology, embedded in the green.

My studio is full of pressed plants and drawings, notes, plant labels. I can organise these materials into timelines. I can keep them still and archive them. My garden, on the other hand, is always threatening to overgrow my organisational attempts—to throw off its labels, to scramble its histories. A rose named after the 1812 war in Canada has been reclaimed by its wild rootstock. During the winter, in a mess of wiry vines, I find it impossible to tell the clematis commemorating the medieval battle of Grunwald, from the clematis honouring the children who died in the Warsaw Uprising. The roots of Waterloo are entwining with Spanish Armada, overshadowing a Russian pilot. Wild mint is taking over! Battle of Britain, a rare floribunda rose which I had grafted from one of the rare remaining specimens held in a nursery in Italy, has made it through another winter on just one spindly stalk. I cannot see it lasting another cold snap.

In 2022 I was invited to develop the Battlefield project for the inner courtyard space of the Kunsthalle Osnabrück, in Lower Saxony. For this, I expanded the collection of plants in the collection to include more than 170 different cultivar varieties, sourced from over 70 nurseries, specialist collectors and botanical gardens, mainly in Europe. This publication indexes all of these plants, and the military events, individuals and paraphernalia after which they were named. It gathers quotes and excerpts from magazines, blogs and online forums of gardeners and gardening enthusiasts speculating upon the origins of these plants, and sharing their experiences of tending to them. It contains traces of the many conversations and collaborations that have nourished this project over the last decade: with the community gardeners at Tempelhofer Feld; with my father whom I often called for garden advice; with curators Anna Voswinckel and Anja Lückenkemper who have nurtured this project over multiple seasons; and with designer Jasper Otto Eisenecker—the 'Hershey' font used in this publication, as well as throughout the Battlefield website and installation signage, was initially developed c.1967 by Dr. Allen Vincent Hershey at the Naval Weapons Laboratory, and was later widely adopted for use in botanical signage. That Jasper sourced a font connected to both weapons development and botany is typical of the detailed care he has brought to this collaboration.

Kunsthalle Osnabrück, winter 2022

History is a continuum. Wars do not occur as isolated, contained incidents— they have repercussions that overflow. In 2015, the disused hangers of the Tempelhofer Feld were transformed into a vast 'arrival centre' for refugees, many of whom had travelled to Germany from Syria, Afghanistan and Iraq. Violent language lies dormant, disarmed by nostalgia for a generation or two, only to re-emerge as dangerous many years later. I think of the 'Iron Cross' oxalis plant, or the 'Victory Salute' phlox, titles evoking Nazi or Red Army militarisations of the 20th century, dangerously reglorified today. In 2024, the Battlefield garden will be planted into the grounds of the Augustaschacht Memorial in Ohrbeck, beside a steelworks building that was used by the Gestapo as a forced labour camp for foreigners during WWII. Next to the garden lie the ruins of a smaller building which, during this period, housed paid German workers of the steelworks. The free workers planted a small cottage garden, raised their children, and, I am told, did not interact with the violence taking place just next door.

Gabriella Hirst

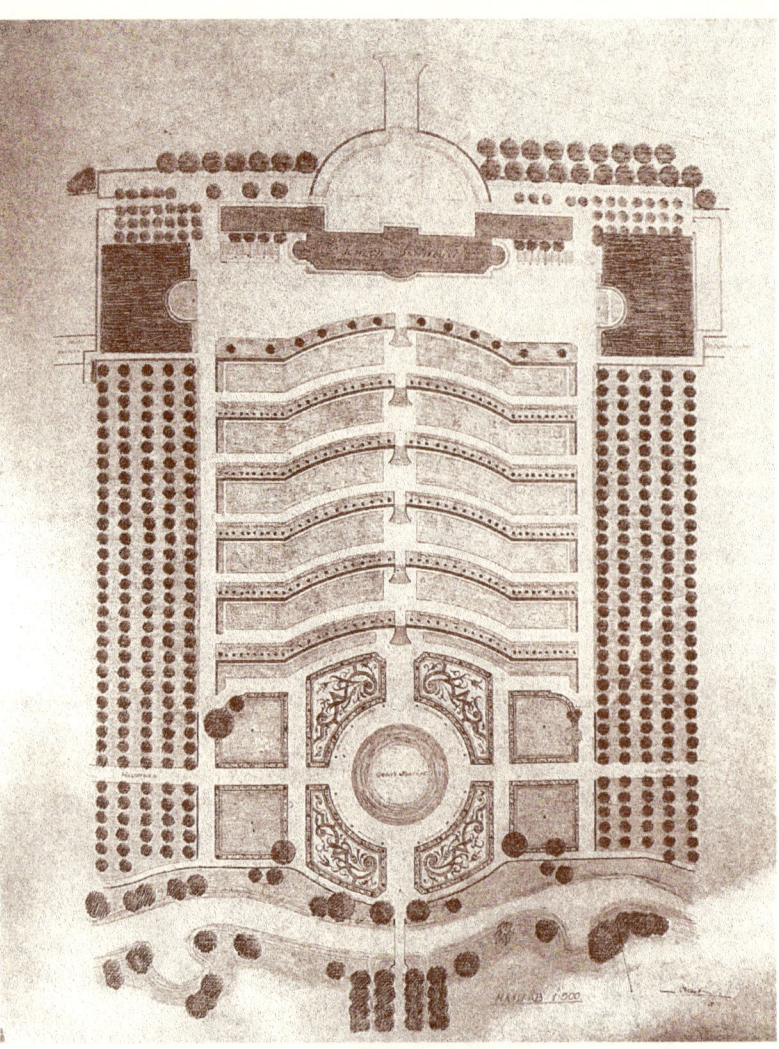

p. 11: Detail 'Walled garden with a woman gardening and others gossiping', from Livre des Prouffits Champetres et Ruraulx by Pietro de Crescenzi, 1230–1320 (vellum).

Camellia 'General George Patton'. Schloss Sanssouci, Potsdam (George Wenzeslaus Knobelsdorff, 1745). Hampton Court, UK (Kip and Knyff's Britannia illustrata, 1708).

p. 13: Hydrangea 'La Marne': sunburnt leaves collected in July 2016.

p. 14: commercial plant passports and ID tags, 2014–2022.

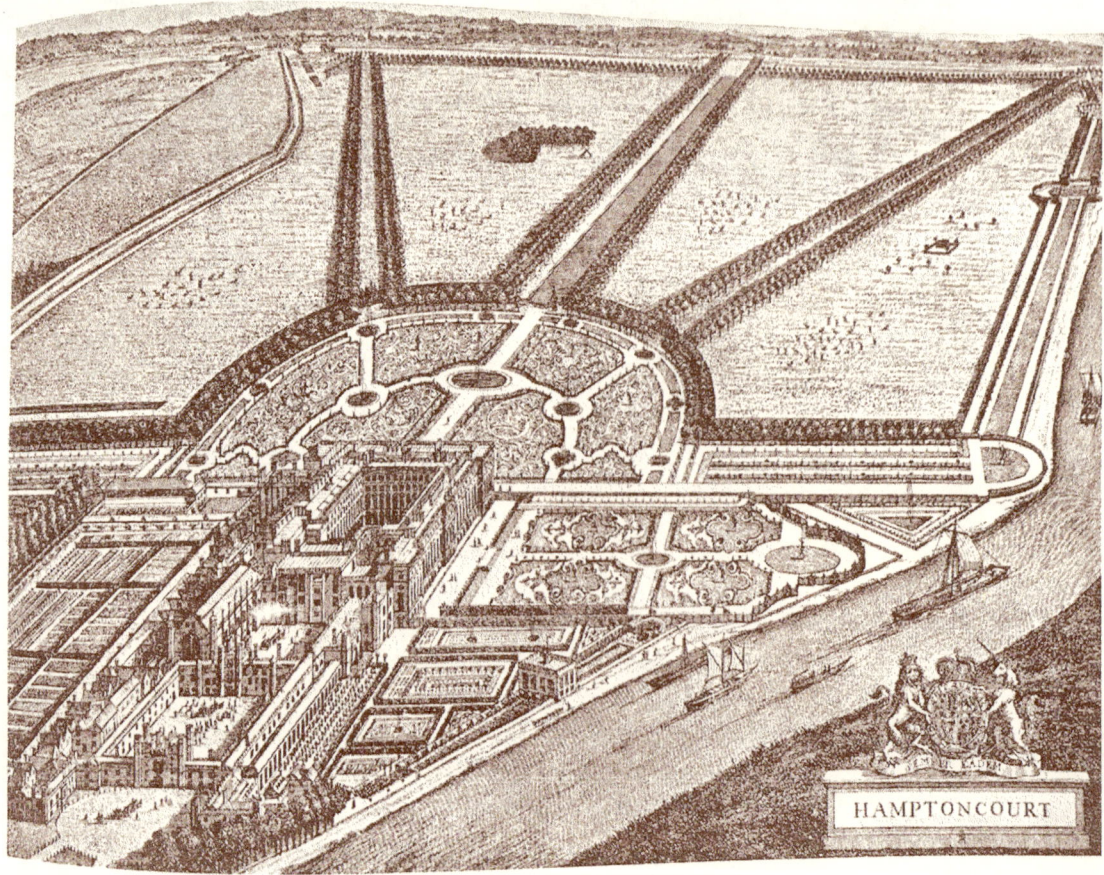

Schloß Hamptoncourt bei London
(Bowles um 1750)

Battlefield-Index
A living collection of plant varieties with names that reference theatres of war

Reads as: cultivar name
common name EN/DE
botanical family
plant hybridiser's name, location and date of registration

Admiral
Poppy Anemone/
Kronen-Anemone
Ranunculaceae
Tubergen, NL,
date unknown

Admiral Ushakov
Gladiolus/Gladiole
Iridaceae
A. Baranov, RU, 2009
Fyodor Ushakov was an 18th Century Russian Naval commander. 'Admiral Ushakov' is also the name of a Sovremenny-class destroyer of the Russian navy in active deployment (2024). • "Powerful gladiolus with a long inflorescence. Champion of the Moscow exhibition 2008 among hybrids."—flowersi.com.ua (Ukr. plant nursery, 2022).

Air Warden
Sweet Pea/Duftwicke
Fabaceae
Thomas Cullen & Sons,
GB, 1942
Air warden = a local civilian officer who supervises defensive measures against war-time air raids. • "This frilly 'Spencer' type was first introduced in 1942. It has a good scent and is ideal for growing up trellis and for cutting."—Mr. Fothergill's seed nursery catalogue.

Alamein
Rose
Rosaceae
Samuel D. McGredy IV,
GB, 1968
The first and second battles of El Alamein, took place in Egypt during WWII.

Alliance Franco-Russe
Rose
Rosaceae
Goinard, FR, 1899
French-Russian Alliance = an economic and military defensive treaty which lasted from 1892–1917.

American Hero
Hosta/Funkie
Asparagaceae
Hansen & Walters Gardens, USA, 2009
Profits from the sale of the 'American Hero' support the charity 'Green Care for Troops', which provides free landscaping services to current USA military veterans. • "Tough and durable like the soldiers it honours"—Greenhouse Growers nursery, USA, 2010.

American Legion
Poppy/Mohnblume
Papaveraceae
W. Wilkes, 1880s,
renamed 1918
Cultivated by Reverend William Wilkes 1880s, renamed by The American Legion after WWI.

American Revolution
Daylily/Taglilie
Asphodelaceae
G. H. Wild, USA, 1972

Amnesty International
Rose
Rosaceae
Guy Delbard, FR, 2007
Named for the international nongovernmental organisation founded in London in 1961, that seeks to publicise violations of the Universal Declaration of Human Rights.

Armada
Hybrid Perpetual Rose
Rosaceae
Harkness Family,
GB, 1988
Named for the 400th anniversary of the Spanish Armada naval conflict.

Armada Pink
Sea Thrift/
Strand-Grasnelke
Plumbaginaceae
Armlee Nurseries,
GB, date unknown
Armada = a fleet of warships.

Armada White
Sea Thrift/
Strand-Grasnelke
Plumbaginaceae
Armlee Nurseries,
GB, date unknown
See above.

Army Nurse
Fuchsia/Fuchsie
Onagraceae
Raymond Hodges,
USA, 1947
Hodges named this "genetically strong and stable" variety to honour the strength of WWII army nurses. • "A real trooper, with excellent form and performance"—USA Army Nurse Corps Association.

Arras
Polyantha Rose
Rosaceae
Eugène Turbat & Co.,
FR, 1924
Battle of Arras, France 1917, WWI. Product possibly marketed for planting atop unmarked graves in Western Front cemeteries.

Arromanches
Hybrid Perpetual Rose
Rosaceae
André Eve, FR, 1975
Named after the site of the Battle of Normandy, 1944.

Atlantic Star
Floribunda Rose
Rosaceae
Gareth Fryer, GB, 1993
Commemorates the 50th anniversary of the Battle of the Atlantic, 1939–1945

Atombombe
Floribunda Rose
Rosaceae
Reimer Kordes,
Federal Republic of Germany, 1953
Named amidst the 'atomic mania' of the Cold War arms race. Marketed as having a colour that would 'strike the eye like an atomic flash'—plant historian Andreas Barlage.

Barricade
Rose
Rosaceae
Maurice Combe,
FR, before 1969
A climbing rose with robust thorny canes and prolific growth.

Battle of Arnhem
Heather/Heidekraut
Ericaceae
I. T. Visser, NL, 1971
A seedling collected near Arnhem by Dr I. T. Visser, registered with this name in commemoration of the 1944 WWII battle.

Battle of Britain
Rose (Hybrid Tea)
Rosaceae
Douglas L. Gandy,
GB, 1970
This rare plant, named after the WWII aerial conflict, has been grafted from one of the few registered existing specimen in the Fineschi gardens, Italy.

Battle of Gettysburg
Daylily/Taglilie
Asphodelaceae
Philip Adams, USA, 1996
"P. Adams (Philip) must be a United States Civil War

enthusiast because all of his daylilies on your list are named after battles in the Civil War (...) many of his other registrations are named after Civil War battles and themes like 'Burning of Atlanta,' 'Emancipation' and 'Atlanta Falls.'"—email exchange with Melodye Campbell, American Hemerocallis Society, 2022.

Big Bertha
Capsicum/
Spanischer Pfeffer
Solanaceae
Petoseed Co., USA, 1978
'Big Bertha' was a howitzer that was first used by the German army in WWI.

Blue Cadet
Hosta/Funkie
Asparagaceae
Paul Aden, USA, 1974
Cadet = a person in training for a military or naval commission.

Bombardier
Pink/Pfingstnelke
Cariophyllaceae
S.T. Byatt,
GB, before 1959
From S.T. Byatt's 'military series'. Bombardier = a crew member who releases bombs from an aircraft.

Bunker Hill
Peony/Pfingstrose
Paeoniaceae
George Hollis, USA, 1904
Battle of Bunker Hill, 1775, American Revolutionary War.
• "See that the weeds do not choke them. Water them if the ground gets very dry, cultivate them thoroughly, and don't lose your enthusiasm, for the end is not yet."—George Hollis. A Manual on the Cultivation and Propagation of Peonies, 1907.

Burma Star
Clematis/Waldrebe
Ranunculaceae
Barry Fretwell, GB, 1990
Named "to honour a relative who endured the pain and privation of the Burma campaign."—Barry Fretwell, hybridiser.

Cambrai
Festubert
Fromelles
Krithia
Le Cateau
Mametz
Ovillers
Passchendaele
Sanctuary Wood
Somme
Vimy Ridge
Auricula
Primulaceae
Richard Austin,
GB, 1980–2000
British hybridiser Richard Austin has developed over 500 different varieties of Auricula since the 1980s. This series was inspired by a trip to western France, visiting WWI battle cemeteries. Now in his 80s, Richard told me that the names of his plants reflect what he is reading or doing at the time the new varieties come through.—GH.

Capitaine Basroger
Moss Rose
Rosaceae
Moreau et Robert,
FR, 1890
"A very high moss rose with light, dark pink to red flowers. Requires a support."
—Schmidt Gartenpflanzen nursery catalogue, 2023.

Capitaine Louis Frère
Hybrid Perpetual Rose
Rosaceae
Alcide Vigneron, FR, 1883
"The plant is named for Captain Louis Frère de Lachaise, a sub-lieutenant in the Seven Years War, as a result of which France lost Canada to England."
—Newsletter of the Heritage Roses Group, Nov 2014.

Capitaine Perrault
Lilac/Flieder
Oleaceae
Victor Lemoine, FR, 1925
Jacques-Nicolas Perrault (1750–1812) was a Canadian civil servant and militia member in Quebec.

Capitaine Thuilleaux
Clematis/Waldrebe
Ranunculaceae
J. Thuilleaux, FR, 1918
Named by nurseryman J. Thuilleaux in remembrance of his son who died in WWI.

Chernobyl
Heather/Heidekraut
Ericaceae
Plaxtol Nurseries,
GB, 1988
Named after the site of the nuclear disaster in the 1986. Cultivar also sold under the name 'Gold Hamilton'.

Colonel de Sansal
Hybrid Perpetual Rose
Rosaceae
Armand Garçon, FR, 1866
Henri-Philippe-Robert Sanson de Sansal (1817–1886) was a French Colonel.

Colonel Fabvier
China Rose
Rosaceae
Jean Laffay, FR,
before 1829
Charles Nicolas Fabvier (1782–1855) was a French general. • "Named after General Fabvier, who fought under Napoleon, and later for Greek independence. Finally he entered Parliament, where he fought the powers of the day against excessive taxation. An admirable Rose and still worth a place."
—E. Bunyard, The Old Book of Roses, 1936.

Combat
Variegated Nettle/
Buntnessel
Lamiaceae
breeder unknown,
free variety.

Commandant Beaurepaire
Gallica Rosa
Rosaceae
Moreau et Robert,
FR, 1864
"Start with a bloom of light pink, add a blaze of bright crimson and stripe with purple-mauve. That will give you an idea, only an idea, of the color combinations the Commandant may display over the growing season."
—Harrison's Antique & Modern Roses, 1984 catalogue.

Commander Hay
Houseleek/
Dach-Hauswurz
Crassulaceae
Len A Earl, GB, 1958
"Commander Hay should have a more sheltered place in your garden and does not tolerate moisture."
—Sempervivum List Hauswurz catalogue, 2022.

Commander in Chief
Fuchsia/Fuchsie
Onagraceae
Rider, USA, 1942
Commander-in-chief = the military rank of the person who holds supreme command of the armed forces, i. e. the President (USA).

Conqueror
Crocus/Krokus
Iridaceae
breeder unknown
Emerges in early spring.

Canna 'General Eisenhower'
"Pink rose commemorates General Jean-Baptiste Kleber", Main Post, 6 October, 2003.

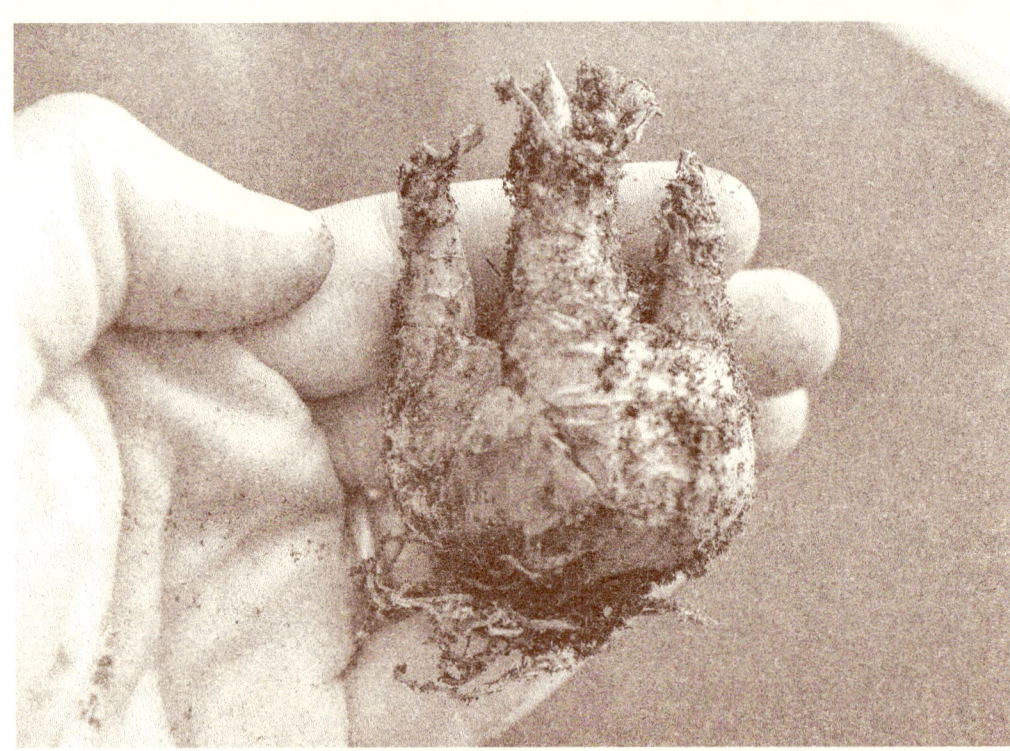

Multiplied bulbs of Narcissus 'Marine Corps'. Echinacea 'Flame Thrower', seed packet, Terra Nova Nursery. Sweetpea 'Air Warden', spring 2022.

pea shoots up "air warden"

Corporal Johann Nagy
Setigera hybrid Rose
Rosaceae
R. Geschwind, Austria-Hungary, 1890
"Healthy, beautiful, vigorous. And what's more, it's scented!"
— blog.staudenundrosen.de

Crusader
Gladiolus/Gladiole
Iridaceae
Carl Fischer, USA, 1976
Crusader = a combatant of the Christian military expeditions to Jerusalem of the 11th, 12th, and 13th centuries.

Dee Day
Wood Anemone/ Busch-Windröschen
Ranunculaceae
Frank Waley, GB, 1918
Small white/purple flowers that herald spring and sleep through summer. Military code designation used for the day of any important invasion or military operation.

Defence Corps
Daffodil/Narzisse
Amaryllidaceae
Brian S. Duncan, Northern Ireland, 1947
In the United Kingdom, The Royal Defence Corps was a division of the British Army formed in 1916 and disbanded in 1936.

Den' Pobedy
Phlox/Flammenblumen
Polemoniaceae
V. Surikova, RU, 2013
"Victory Salute" (tr. RU). Russian holiday that commemorates the victory over Nazi Germany in 1945.

Desert Storm
Daffodil/Narzisse
Amaryllidaceae
Clive Postles, GB, 1991
Operation Desert Storm, the primary US military operation of the Gulf War (1991).

Deuil du Colonel Denfert
Hybrid Perpetual Rose
Rosaceae
Jacques-Julien Margottin, FR, 1878
Pierre Denfert-Rochereau (1823—1878) was a colonel in the Franco-Prussian war.

Deutsches Danzig
Polyantha Rose
Rosaceae
Peter Lambert, German Reich, 1935
"German Danzig" (tr. DE). In 1939, Nazi German troops invaded the Polish city of Danzig (Gdansk).

Dunkirk
Hybrid Tea Rose
Rosaceae
Alexander Dickson III, GB, 1947
Named after the Dunkirk evacuation in 1940.

Dzieci Warszawy
Clematis/Waldrebe
Ranunculaceae
Władysław Noll, Polish People's Republic, 1987
"Children of Warsaw" (tr. PL). Commemorates the young participants of the Warsaw Uprising, 1944.

Falklands
Fuchsia/Fuchsie
Onagraceae
Harry Dunnett, GB, 1984
Name likely refers to the 1982 war waged between Britain and Argentina over the Falklands Islands. •
"I can't think of any plants named after battles. Not really the most appropriate association, I should think, though there seem to be plenty named after military personnel."
—email exchange, Katharine Murray, Sundial Nursery, UK.

Flame Thrower
Dahlia/Dahlie
Asteraceae
Nick Gitts, USA, 2011

Flame Thrower
Echinacea/Sonnenhut
Asteraceae
H. Korlipara, USA, 2011

Flame Thrower
Variegated Nettle/ Buntnessel
Lamiaceae
Ball Horticultural Co., USA, 2018

Foreign Legion
Tall Bearded Iris/ Deutsche Schwertlilie
Iridaceae
Keith Keppel, USA, 2000
"Sensitive to wind and harsh sunlight."—private iris supplier.

Friendly Fire
Tall Bearded Iris/ Deutsche Schwertlilie
Iridaceae
Keith Keppel, USA, 2002
"One of the most difficult processes of marketing a plant is finding a name which somehow gives some feeling of its color or overall ambiance (...) Friendly Fire has (...) a pleasant enough blue, with a bright fiery red beard."—Keith Keppel, iris hybridiser.

Friendly Fire
Fuchsia/Fuchsie
Onagraceae
Jack Caunt, GB, 1985

Fusilier
Pink/Pfingstnelke
Cariophyllaceae
S.T. Byatt, GB, before 1955
Historically, a fusilier is a soldier equipped with a fusil, a type of flintlock musket. The Royal Regiment of Fusiliers is an infantry regiment of the British Army.

Gallipoli Centenary Rose
Rose
Rosaceae
Reimer Kordes, DE, 2000
Originally named by Kordes as 'Jugendliebe' ("young love", tr. DE) in 2000, later introduced in South Africa by Ludwig's Roses in 2008 as 'Archbishop Desmond Tutu' and recently in Australia by Treloar Roses in 2015 as 'Gallipoli Centenary Rose', referencing the Gallipoli campaign, 1915—1916.

Gastello
Lilac/Flieder
Oleaceae
Leonid Kolesnikov, UdSSR, 1946
Nikolai Gastello (1907—1941) was a Soviet military pilot and war hero of the USSR.

Géant des Batailles
Hybrid Perpetual Rose
Rosaceae
Antoine Nérard, FR, 1845
Named to commemorate the Battle of Borodino in 1812. 'The Giant of Battles' is a reference to Napoleon, who commanded the French forces.

Géant des Batailles
Oleander
Apocynaceae
Félix Sahut, FR, 1898
See above. Often sold in garden centres under the alternative name "Revenge".

Général Bedeau
Hybrid Perpetual Rose
Rosaceae
Jacques-Julien Margottin, FR, 1851
Marie Alphonse Bedeau (1804—1863) was a French general and minister, who took part in several military campaigns in French-occupied Northern Africa.

Général Clerc
Rose
Rosaceae
Portemer fils, FR, 1859
Vicomte Antoine-Marguerite Clerc (1774–1846) was a general in the Revolutionary and Royal armies of France.

Général Drouot
Moss Rose
Rosaceae
Jean-Pierre Vibert, FR, 1847
General Antoine Drouot (1774–1847) was a war minister to Napoleon.

General Eisenhower
Canna
Cannaceae
C. L. Sprenger, Damman et Cie, Kingdom of Italy, 1898
"We have Canna 'General Eisenhower' in our collection, under its original name of 'La France'. US nurseries renamed it to honour their president, and increase sales! (...) The breeder was Karl Sprenger, an Austrian running his nursery, Dammans et Cie, alongside Mount Vesuvius in Italy. He bred a new type of canna (Italian Group) in the 1890s, and named many after European countries, i.e. Italia, Alemania, Austria, America. The nursery was destroyed when Vesuvius erupted again about 1905. Sprenger was reputed internationally and was then appointed by Kaiser Wilhelm to establish the gardens at his Adriatic summer palace. Sprenger was killed in WWI in bad circumstances."—email exchange with Thor Dalebö, 22 February, 2022.

General George Patton
Camellia/Kamelie
Theaceae
Coolidge Nursery, USA, 1946
George Smith Patton Jr. (1885–1945) was a general in the United States Army during WWII.

Général Hoche
Fuchsia/Fuchsie
Onagraceae
Victor Lemoine, FR, 1886
Louis Lazare Hoche (1768–1797) was a French soldier who served during the French Revolutionary Wars and rose to become a general of the Revolutionary Army.

Général Jacqueminot
Hybrid Perpetual Rose
Rosaceae
Rousselet, FR, 1853
"One of Napoleon's favorite officers caught his own daughter in the arms of a young Officer and stabbed the boy to death (...) In the arbor where the lovers had been seated under a large pink rose bush, there appeared a short time afterward a stem, deep red and quite different from the original rose." Sean Mccan, The Ultimate Rose Book, 1993.

Général Kléber
Centifolia/Moss Rose
Rosaceae
Moreau et Robert, FR, 1856
Jean-Baptiste Kléber (1753–1800) was a French General. While serving as administrator for Egypt, he was stabbed to death by Suleiman al-Halabi, a Syrian-born 23 year old theology student. Al-Halabi's motives are variously recorded as fanaticism or as local revolt against the foreign colonising occupation. Al-Halabi was tortured and publicly executed.

Général Labutère
Rose
Rosaceae
breeder unknown
Most likely references French Général de Labossière (1775–1809).

Général Leclerc
Pear/Kultur-Birne
Rosaceae
Charles-Alfred Nomblot, FR, 1954
Philippe François Marie Leclerc de Hauteclocque was a French general during WWII.

General MacArthur
Hybrid Tea Rose
Rosaceae
Edward Gurney Hill, USA, 1904
Arthur MacArthur Jr. (1845–1912) was an American lieutenant general and military governor of the Philipines.

Général MacMahon
Peony/Pfingstrose
Paeoniaceae
Jacques Calot, FR, 1867
Patrice de MacMahon (1808–1893) was a French general and politician, and Governor General of Algeria.

Général Monk
Fuchsia/Fuchsie
Onagraceae
Auguste Miellez, FR, date unknown
Likely named after General Monck, an English soldier, who fought during the Wars of the Three Kingdoms, a series of conflicts fought 1639 to 1653 between and within England, Scotland and Ireland.

General Montgomery
Astilbe/Prachtspiere
Saxifragaceae
Kooy, GB, 1948
General Montgomery was a Senior British Army officer who participated in WWI, the Irish War of Independence and WWII.

General Patton
Gladiolus/Gladiole
Iridaceae
Hobby, 1996
"I had (General Patton) for two seasons. I threw it out because of lack of vitality and bad growing habits. I think some growers can have it, but probably with viruses inside (...) I do not recommend buying this cultivar. It will be disappointing to grow."—email exchange with Petr Šmída, gladiolus hybridiser, 2022.

General Pershing
Lilac/Flieder
Oleaceae
Victor Lemoine, FR, 1924
General of the US Armies, John Joseph Pershing (1860–1948).

General Pershing
Oleander
Apocynaceae
breeder unknown
General Pershing is vulnerable to aphids, which can be removed by hand, or with a treatment of nettle and water.

Général Schablikine
Tea Rose
Rosaceae
Gilbert Nabonnand, FR, 1878
Russian general Ivan Pavlovitch Schablikine (1809–1888) spent his holidays near the Nabonnand nursery in France.

General Sheridan
Lilac/Flieder
Oleaceae
John Dunbar, USA, 1917
Philip Henry Sheridan was a career United States Army officer and Union general (1831–1888), who fought in the American Frontier Wars and in the American Civil War.

General Sikorski
Clematis/Waldrebe
Ranunculaceae
Bruder Stefan Franczak, Polish People's Republic, before 1975
Wladyslaw Eugeniusz Sikorski (1881–1943) was a Polish general and politician.

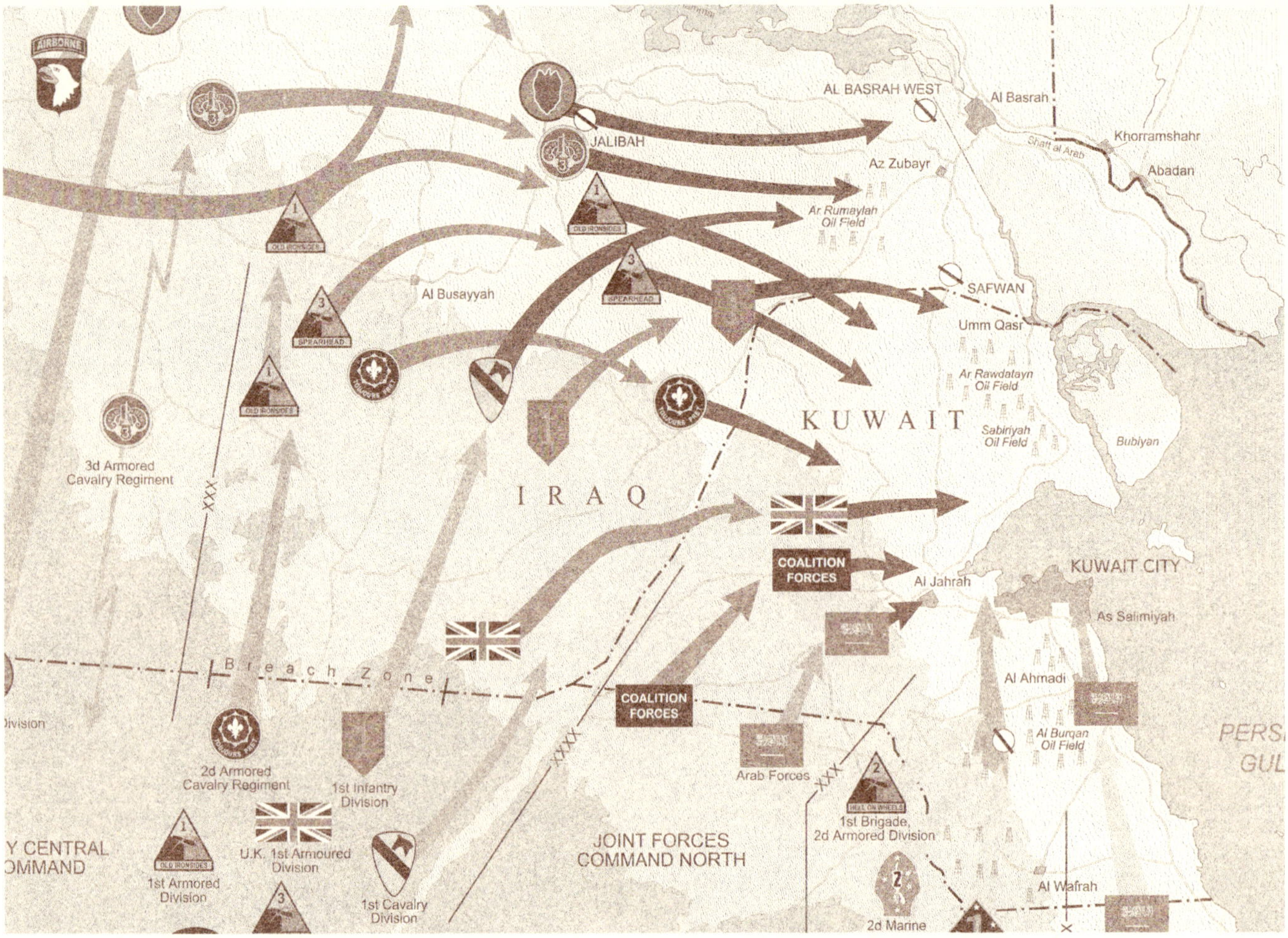

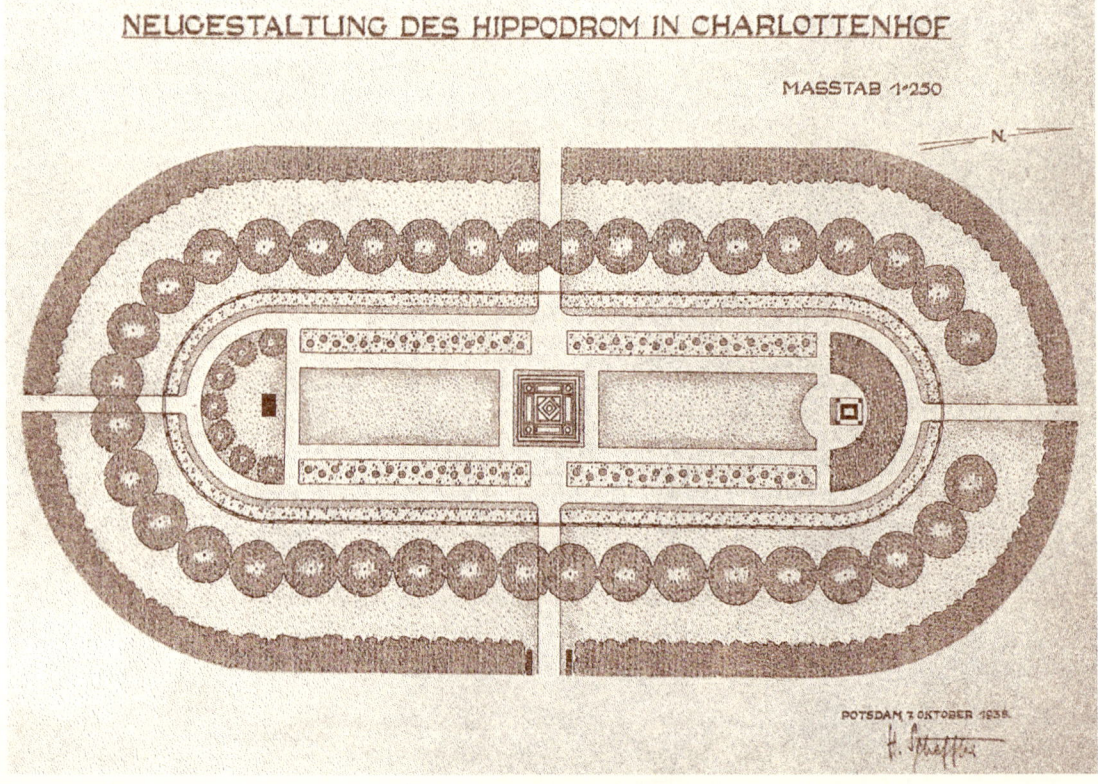

p. 21: Rosa 'Waterloo', pressing made 2019.

Troop movements, Operation Desert Shield/Storm 1990–1991.
Hippodrom in Charlottenhoff (Sanssouci, Potsdam), Aesthetik der GartenKunst. Lothar Abel, Wien, 1877.
Rosa 'Armada', member comment on helpmefind.com/roses.

Initial post 25 FEB 04 by Unregistered Guest

Armada is perhaps my favorite rose, but beware of the thorns!

Général Stefánik
Hybrid Perpetual Rose
Jan Böhm,
Czechoslovakia, 1931
Milan Rastislav Stefánik (1880—1919) was a Slovak politician, diplomat and general who was War Minister for Czechoslovakia during WWI. • "When it was smaller, I remember it as being so spectacular when in flower—covered with medium-sized blooms. Now, the blooms are much smaller, and less abundant; I suspect that the plant has become 'too big for its britches', as it were. My idea for this year was to cut it way back after it blooms—but by how much?"—member comment, 17 May 2020, helpmefind.com/roses/generalstefanik

Général Tétard
Hybrid Wichurana Rose
Rosaceae
Pajotin-Chédane,
FR, 1918
"At the Pajotin-Chedanne establishments a dozen bombs fell in a nursery and particularly in one of the squares of roses for sale, 9.000 roses were totally destroyed."—Les Amis des Roses, 1947.

General Wavell
Rhododendron
Ericaceae
C. Ingram, GB, 1952
Archibald Percival Wavell (1883—1950) was a Field Marshall of the British army who took part in the Second Boer War and WWI, and was titled Commander-in-Chief of British occupied India from 1941—1943. • Requires acidic (ericaceous) soil.

General Wavell
Fuchsia/Fuchsie
Onagraceae
H. H. Whiteman,
GB, 1942
See above.

Generale Vicomtesse de Vibraye
Hydrangea/Hortensie
Hydrangeaceae
Emil Moullière, FR, 1909
"'Generale Vicomtesse de Vibraye' is a noble beauty that presents itself with great flower colors from pink to blue to violet."—product information, www.annas-garten.de

Gentleman at Arms
Daffodil/Narzisse
Amaryllidaceae
breeder unknown, 2016
The Honourable Corps of Gentlemen at Arms is a bodyguard to the British Monarchy.

Grenade
Tall Bearded Iris/
Deutsche Schwertlilie
Iridaceae
Cayeux, FR, 2008
The German common name for this plant, 'Schwertlilie' (sword lily), refers to the shape of new foliage protruding through the soil.

Grenadier
Pelargonium/Pelargonie
Geraniaceae
W. Bull, GB, 1872
Traditionally, a specialist soldier who threw hand grenades in battle.

Grunwald
Clematis/Waldrebe
Ranunculaceae
Szczepan Marczyński,
PL, 2014
The Battle of Grunwald, 1410, saw the defeat of German-Prussian Teutonic knights by Polish-Lithuanian military forces.

Iron Cross
Four-leaved wood-sorrel/
Vierblättriger Sauerklee
Oxalidaceae
W. Blokker, NL, 1969
Named due to purple marks in the center of leaves "resembling the Iron Cross military medal" (Gynelle Leon). This name has fallen out of favour due to far-right associations of the Iron Cross.

Kapitän
Austrian Speedwell/
Österreichischer Ehrenpreis
Scrophulariaceae
breeder unknown
"Captain" (tr. DE)

La Marne
Hydrangea/Hortensie
Hydrangeaceae
Emil Moullière, FR, 1917
First Battle of the Marne, France 1914. • "Bushy and rigid character, the flowers do not collapse to the ground."

La Marne
Polyantha Rose
Rosaceae
Barbier Frères & Co.,
FR, 1915
"Named for the First Battle of the Marne, fought early September 1914, which halted the German advance thirty miles from Paris. It is an excellent polyantha with pink ruffled petals glowing in the center, the flowers massed in loose clusters."—Darrell G. H. Schramm, Roses of WWI, 2014.

La Somme
Pernetiana Rose
Rosaceae
Barbier Frères & Co,
FR, 1919
Named in reference to the WWI Battle of the Somme, 1916.

Lord Lieutenant
Anemone/
Kronen-Anemone
Ranunculaceae
Tubergen,
NL, date unknown.
A Lord Lieutenant is the British monarch's personal representative in each lieutenancy area of the United Kingdom. Historically, each lieutenant was responsible for organising the county's militia.

Loyalist
Daffodil/Narzisse
Amaryllidaceae
J. Lionel Richardson,
Irish Free State/
Saorstát Éireann, 1923
The Irish Civil War was fought between 1922 and 1923. In an Irish context, Loyalists support the continued existence of Northern Ireland within the United Kingdom. • "Loyalist" bulbs multiply underground from energy drawn in via late summer foliage, remaining dormant throughout winter.

Loyalist
Hosta/Funkie
Asparagaceae
G. Van Eijk-Bos & Walters Gardens,
USA/NL, 1998
The Hostas 'Patriot', 'Loyalist', 'Revolution', and 'American Hero', all named in reference to the American Revolutionary War (1775—1783), were bred sequentially from one another's growth.

Magenta
Astilbe/Prachtspiere
Saxifragaceae
Victor Lemoine,
FR, 19th C
"I also have an Astilbe called Magenta which is named after the battle of Magenta during the Crimean War. It is named after the battle and not the colour Magenta as it is a purple coloured flower."—John Ashley, National Astilbe Collection Registrar, UK.

Mandatory Evacuation
Daylily/Taglilie
Asphodelaceae
Chris Rogers, USA/NL, 2004

Maréchal Davoust
Moss Rose
Rosaceae
Robert et Moreau, FR, 1853
Louis-Nicolas Davout (1770–1823) was a French Napoleonic Marshal.

Maréchal Foch
Grape Vine/Weinrebe
Vitaceae
Eugène Kuhlmann, FR, 1911
This variety was established in 1911 and named "Kuhlmann 188-2", after its breeder, Eugène Kuhlmann. It was renamed upon its market release in 1921 after the French WWI Supreme Allied Commander, Ferdinand Foch (1851–1929). Foch was widely condemned in Germany for his role in WWI armistice conditions, the vine's renaming possibly played a revanchist role in the prohibition of the cultivation of this variety in Germany in the mid-1930s.

Maréchal Foch
Hydrangea/Hortensie
Hydrangeaceae
Emil Moullière, FR, 1924
Can cause mild stomach upset if ingested and contact with foliage may aggravate skin allergies.

Maréchal Foch
Lilac/Flieder
Oleaceae
Victor Lemoine, FR, 1924
See above.

Maréchal Foch
Polyantha Rose
Rosaceae
Ernest Levavasseur, FR, 1918
See above.

Maréchal Lannes
Lilac/Flieder
Oleaceae
Victor Lemoine, FR, 1910
Named after Jean Lannes, Duc de Montebello (1769–1809), a Marshal of Napoleon's army.

Maréchal MacMahon
Pelargonium/Pelargonie
Geraniaceae
breeder unknown, FR, 1862.
Patrice Maurice de MacMahon, was a French General and political figure, who participated in the French conquest of Algeria (1827–1857), the Crimean War (1853–1856), the Franco-Austrian War (1859), and the Franco-Prussian War (1870–1871). See also Peony 'Général MacMahon'.

Maréchal Niel
Tea Rose
Rosaceae
Louis Castel, FR, 1857
Adolphe Niel (1802–1869) was a French Army general and statesman.

Margaret Thatcher
Gladiolus/Gladiole
Iridaceae
Petr Šmída, CZ, 2022
"I can only inform you about my variety Margaret Thatcher. I am 37 years old, so I have not experienced her political career as British Prime Minister, but I have read her book and respect her as a right-wing and conservative politician whose voice is missing from the current madness. I respect her as a charismatic and intelligent woman and I realise that there is no longer any political figure of her calibre. I have therefore dedicated to her at least my pink gladiolus, which I selected in 2014, which I think is of great quality."—email exchange with Petr Šmída, gladiolus hybridiser.

Marine Corps
Daffodil/Narzisse
Amaryllidaceae
Nial Watson, Northern Ireland, 2000
Marine Corps refers to the part of the U.S. military that consists of soldiers who serve at sea and also on land. • Over the summer, once blooms and some foliage has faded, Daffodil bulbs split and multiply underground.

Marschall Vasilevskij
Lilac/Flieder
Oleaceae
Leonid Kolesnikov, UdSSR, 1963
Aleksandr Vasilevsky (1895–1977) was a Soviet Marshal. 'Marshall Vasilevsky' is also the name of a Russian offshore military support vessel, built in 2018 and currently deployed in the Baltic Sea (2024).

Marschall Žukov
Lilac/Flieder
Oleaceae
Leonid Kolesnikov, UdSSR, 1948
Georgy Konstantinovich Zhukov (1896–1974), was Marshal of the Soviet Union. Leonid Kolesnikov was a celebrated lilac breeder from the Soviet Union. He participated in both World Wars, including, allegedly, as a driver for Marshal Zhukov. Kolesnikov received the Stalin Prize in 1958 for his contributions to horticulture.

Megiddo
Floribunda Rose
Rosaceae
Douglas L. Gandy, GB, 1970
Name could refer to either the 1918 battle between the British and Ottoman Empires, or to one of two previous battles on the same site.

Merchant Marine
Tall Bearded Iris/Deutsche Schwertlilie
Iridaceae
Keith Keppel, USA, 2006
Merchant Marine = the commercial ships of a nation, whether privately or publicly owned. Whilst not deployed specifically for military purpose, they often play support/crossover roles in naval operations and staffing.

Monte Cassino
Clematis/Waldrebe
Ranunculaceae
Bruder Stefan Franczak, PL, 1990
Commemorates Polish involvement in the 1944 Battle for Monte Cassino, Italy.

Monte Cassino
Aster/Myrthenaster
Asteraceae
breeder unknown
For the Battle of Monte Cassino, see above.

Partizanka
Lilac/Flieder
Oleaceae
Bibikova & Smolskii, UdSSR, 1964
"This very rare lilac variety comes from the Belarusian breeding tradition. The two breeders Smolskii and Bibikova created this variety in 1964 and named it after female partisans during World War II."—Fliedertraum nursery.

Patriot
Hosta/Funkie
Asparagaceae
John Machen Jr, USA, 1991
These hostas, named in reference to the American Revolutionary War (1775–1783). See also hosta 'Loyalist'.

p. 24, 25:
Camellia 'General George Patton'
Hydrangea 'Generale Vicomtesse de Vibraye'
Rosa 'Général Labutère'
Common Lilac 'General Pershing'
Clematis 'General Sikorski'
Oleander 'General Pershing'
Rosa 'Commandant Beaurepaire'
Fuchsia 'General Wavell'
Common Pear 'Général Leclerc'
Rosa 'Général Stefánik'
Rosa 'Général Drouot'
Fuchsia 'Général Monk'
Rosa 'Général Bedeau'
Rosa 'Général Clerc'
Peony 'Général MacMahon'
Rosa 'Général Jacqueminot'
Rosa 'Général Schablikine'
Rosa 'General MacArthur'
Rosa 'Général Gallieni'
Pelargonium 'Maréchal MacMahon'
Hydrangea 'Maréchal Foch'
Rosa 'Général Kléber'
Gladiolus 'Admiral Ushakov'
Clematis 'Capitaine Thuilleaux'
Rosa 'Maréchal Davoust'

Espalier study, from 'Die Obst- und Traubenzucht', R. Goethe, 1900.
Troop positions, Battle of Borodino, Sept 9, 1812, United States Military Academy Department of History, 2009.

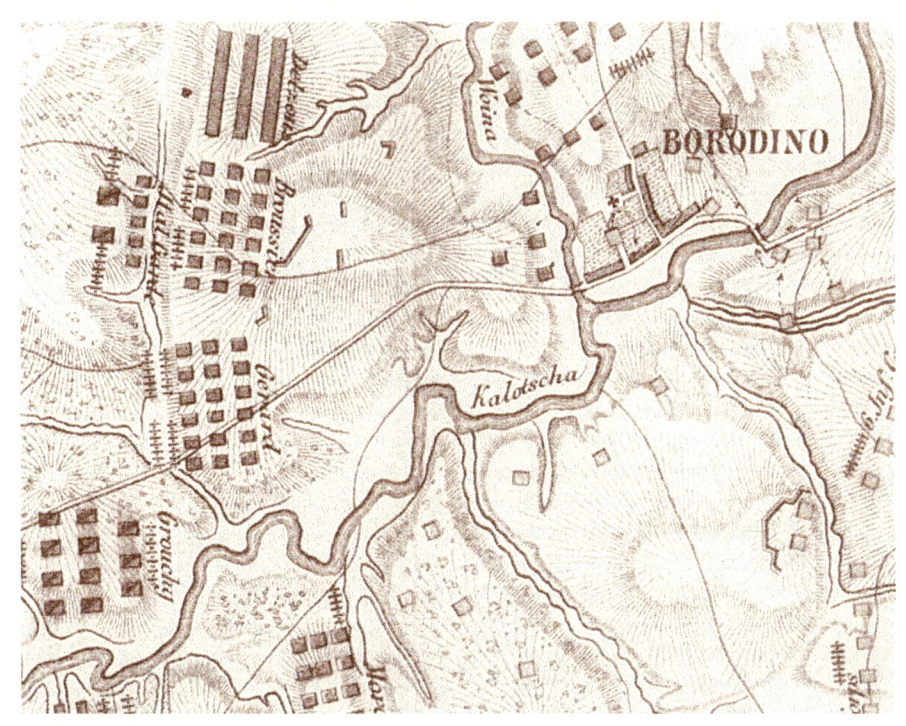

Fig. 3.
Unrichtig gezogene Verrier=Palmette, welche zeigt, wie die der Stammlinie zunächst stehenden obersten und jüngsten Baumteile sich viel stärker entwickeln, als die unteren seitlich von dieser Linie stehenden, wenn nicht durch richtigen Schnitt ein Ausgleich geschaffen wird.

Rose 'Deutsches Danzig'.
Member comment, 'Deutsches Danzig', helpmefind.com/roses
Clematis 'Warszawska Nike', label, Baumschule Horstmann, 2020.
Rose 'Atlantic Star', sketch, 2017.

p. 29: Clematis 'Westerplatte', vines collected 2021.

Initial post 5 SEP 11 by sam w

Judging from its date, this rose was probably named to honor (!) the Nazi/Nationalist goal of claiming the Free City of Danzig, a culturally German but geographically Polish city on the sea, which was established by the League of Nations. In 1933 the Nazi party took control and eliminated all democratic opposition; in 1939, the city was absorbed into the German Reich where it remained until liberation. Such an unpleasant set of associations for such a cute little rose!

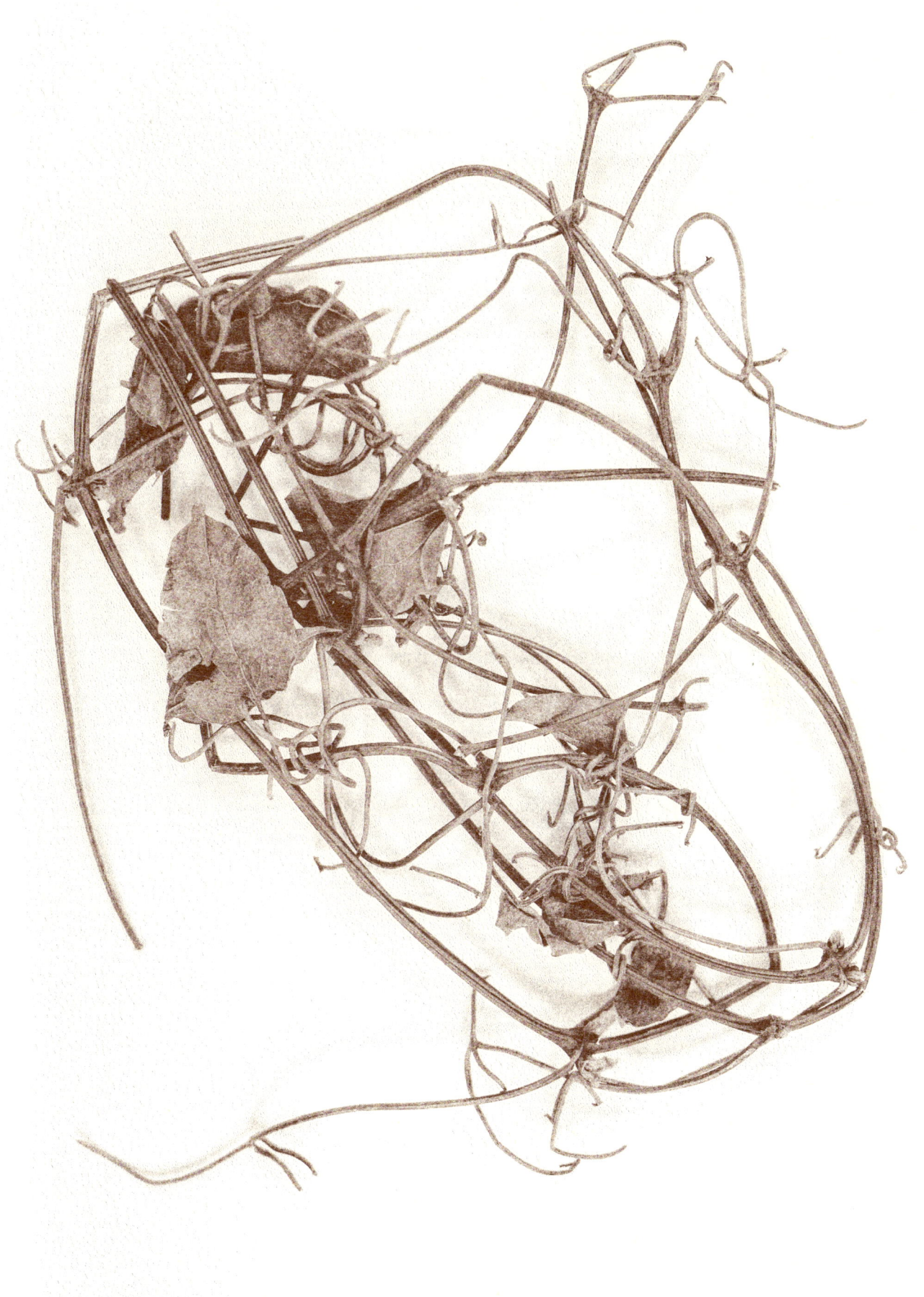

Perestroika
Heather/Heidekraut
Ericaceae
Kurt Kramer, DE,
before 1998
This heather was "named Perestroika in consultation with my Dutch and British colleagues in recognition of the work of Mikhail Gorbachev."—Kurt Kramer, heather hybridiser.

Power Grenade
Houseleek/
Dach-Hauswurz
Crassulaceae
Vitroflora, Republic of Poland, PL,
date unknown

Preemptive Strike
Daylily/Taglilie
Asphodelaceae
E. Scott, USA, 2002
"Back in 2002, the year it was registered, U. S. President George W. Bush came up with a Preemptive Strike policy. It was after the Sept. 11 2001 attacks. That could be the source of the name. Preemptive Strike is also the title of a Star Trek: The Next Generation episode so that could also be the origin of the name." email exchange with Melodye Campbell, American Hemerocallis Society, 2022.

R. A. F. (Royal Air Force)
Fuchsia/Fuchsie
Onagraceae
Gordon Garson,
USA, 1942
Named in honour of the British Royal Air Force. • During WWII, 'Gardening' was standard R. A. F. slang for sowing mines in rivers, ports and oceans from low heights, possibly because each sea area around the European coasts was given a code-name of flowers or vegetables.

Rahvarinne
Clematis/Waldrebe
Ranunculaceae
Uno Kivistik,
USSR/Estonian SSR,
1985
Breeder Uno Kivistik, named this Clematis 'Rahvarinne', which is the name of the political movement against Soviet rule in Estonia during the 1980s.

Red Admiral
Begonia/Begonie
Begoniaceae
Blackmore & Langdon,
GB, 1960

Red Admiral
Phlox/Flammenblumen
Polemoniaceae
Inshriach Nurseries,
SC, 1968

Red Army
Amarant/Dreifarbiger Fuchsschwanz
Amaranthaceae
breeder unknown
The Workers' and Peasants' Red Army, often shortened to the Red Army, was the army and air force of the Russian Soviet Federative Socialist Republic and, after 1922, the Union of Soviet Socialist Republics.

Red Army
Sneezeweed/
Sonnenbraut
Asteraceae
Coen Jansen, NL, 2010
See above.

Red Baron
Sweetgrass
Poaceae
breeder unknown
Named after Manfred Albrecht Freiherr von Richthofen, known as Baron von Richthofen or the Red Baron, a fighter pilot with the German Air Force during WWI.

Red Missile
Capsicum/
Spanischer Pfeffer
Solanaceae
breeder and date unknown

Roter Oktober
Heather/Heidekraut
Ericaceae
D. Scholjegerdes, GB, 1987
"Red October" (tr. DE) is another name for the October Revolution of 1917, an armed uprising of the socialist Bolshevik party in Saint Petersburg, Russia. • Autumn blooming variety with red-coloured blossoms.

Royal Navy
Hyacinth/Hyazinthe
Hyacinthaceae
J.S. Pennings, GB, 2012
Named in reference to the United Kingdom's naval warfare force.

Saliut Pobedy
Clematis/Waldrebe
Ranunculaceae
M. Beskaravainaya,
UkrSSR, 1971
"Salute to Victory" (tr. RU)

Samourai
Apricot/Aprikose
Rosaceae
Pépinières Escande,
FR, 2012
Hereditary military caste of medieval and early-modern Japan from the late 12th century until their abolition in 1876.

Sebastopol
Fuchsia/Fuchsie
Onagraceae
Michael Pennisi,
USA, 1968
Possibly named in reference to the WWII Siege of Sevastopol, a military engagement fought between Germany and Romania against the Soviet Union for control of Sevastopol, a port in the Crimea, 1941–1942.

Siegesperle
Polyantha Rose
Hermann Kiese,
German Empire, 1915
"Victory Pearl" (tr. DE).
Named by German rose breeder Kiese at the start of WWI. It is seldom available for purchase. • "In 1915 Kiese gave a creamy white polyantha the name 'Siegesperle', and after a world shattered, in 1920 he christened one of his last cultivars 'Deutsche Hoffnung'."—Anny Jakob, The Finnish Rose Society, 1976

Silent Sentry
Daylily/Taglilie
Asphodelaceae
Jeff Salter, USA, 1992
Sentry = a soldier standing guard at a point of passage.

Soldier Boy
Rose
Rosaceae
E. Burton Le Grice,
GB, 1953
In the UK, the National Service Act was implemented in 1949, requiring all 'healthy males' aged 17 to 21 to serve in the armed forces for 18 months, and remain on the reserve list for four years.

Solferino
Astilbe/Prachtspiere
Saxifragaceae
Victor Lemoine, FR, 1910
Named in reference to the Battle of Solferino, fought in 1859 between the Franco-Sardinian Alliance and the Austrian army, during the Second Italian War of Independence.

Solferino
Pelargonium/Pelargonie
Geraniaceae
Arthur Langley-Smith,
GB, 1968
See above.

HYBRIDIST......AND AUTHOR

HYBRIDIZER L.A. KOLESNIKOV AND 'Miechta'

Amateur floriculturist L. Kolesnikov has won the Stalin Prize for breeding new strains of lilac. His garden in Moscow holds about 500 kinds of lilac, including more than 300 new ones of his own breeding.

L. A. KOLESNIKOV

....A TRIBUTE TO 80 YEARS AND STILL

Phlox paniculata 'Den Pobedy'

€ 8.50

including 13% VAT.

(RUS)

The red of this newer Russian variety can be described as one of the very few true red tones available, a deep, warm, dark blood red. The name translates to "Victory Day" in German. Actually, politics should have no place in plant names, especially not from past, unfortunate times and especially not in the current situation. But those who love perennials have no boundaries or nationalisms in their heads. In any case, 'Den Pobedy' is one of the absolute top varieties that we don't want to be without!

Delivery time: March - June / September - November

Add to Cart

Categories: Bedding and wild perennials, Phlox paniculata - phlox, tall summer phlox

Russian Embassy in USA 🇷🇺
@RusEmbUSA
Russia government organization

🕊 On May 9️⃣, Russian diplomats, as part of the international action 🌍 "Garden of Memory", planted lilac 🌸 bushes on the territory of the Embassy, which will remind future generations of the heroism of the heroes who won the #GreatPatrioticWar
🕊
facebook.com/RusEmbUSA/post...

MFA Russia 🇷🇺 and 6 others

10:53 pm · 9 May 2021 · Twitter Web App

17 Retweets   77 Likes

Newsletter of the International Lilac Society, Vol. 2, No. 2 Convention Issue, 1973.
'Sarasto Stauden' nursery online catalogue, July 2022.
[Tweet] Russian Embassy in USA, @RusEmbUSA, 10.53 pm—9 May 2021.

Rose 'Arras', sketch, 2015. Pelargoniums, Buckingham Palace, found postcard, 2022. "Geraniums have been branded vulgar—but they shouldn't be relegated to the compost heap yet", Padraic Flanagan, www.inews.co.uk, 23 April 2021.

p. 33: Rose 'Battle of Britain', pressing made 2020

Despite his dismissal, fans abound of the cheery, resilient geranium – or, to use its proper name, pelargonium. And in the highest echelons too. The Queen, reportedly, has insisted on seeing scarlet geraniums on the island at the front of Buckingham Palace. The variety had to be the fire-engine red and aptly-named Grenadier geranium to guarantee a suitably majestic display.

Nr. 964. Siegesperle.

Rose 'Siegesperle', (tr. DE, Victory Pearl), Hermann Kiese, Deutschland, 1915, Blumenschmidt catalogue, 1929.
Peony 'Victoire de La Marne' (tr. FR, Victory of the Marne), Dessert & Méchin, France, 1915, pressing made 2018.

Iris 'Foreign Legion', sketch, April 2022.
Daylily 'Preemptive Strike', online catalogue, www.taglilienshop.de, 2022.
Peony 'Bunker Hill', Horticulture magazine, Biodiversity Heritage Library, 1905.

p. 37: Fuchsia 'Falklands', pressing made 2021.

Solidarność
Clematis/Waldrebe
Ranunculaceae
Szczepan Marczyński,
PL, 2003

"Solidarity" (tr. PL). Polish trade union and political organisation instrumental in the 1989–1990 revolution.

Souvenir de Malmedy
Gallica Rose
John Scarman, DE, 1996

Possibly named in memory of the Malmedy massacre. In 1944, German Waffen-SS soldiers murdered eighty-four USA prisoners of war near the Belgian city of Malmedy.

Spanish Conquest
Dahlia/Dahlie
Asteraceae
K. E. Stock, USA, 2005

The Spanish-Aztec War was one of the primary events in the Spanish colonisation of the Americas, commencing in 1519. The Dahlia, or Acocoxochitle as they are called in Nahuatl, is the contemporary state flower of Mexico. Hybridiser K. Stock's other plants for 2008 included 'Spanish Soldier', 'Mayan Pearl', and 'Mayan Blood'.

Spitfire
Heather/Heidekraut
Ericaceae
R. E. Hardwick, GB, 1955

The Supermarine Spitfire is a British single-seat fighter aircraft introduced in 1938.

Spitfire
Peruvian Lily/Inka-Lilie
Alstroemeriaceae
breeder unknown, 1960s

See above.

Squadron Leader
Fuchsia/Fuchsie
Onagraceae
Edwin Goulding,
GB, 1986

"We have a Squadron Leader fuchsia that we were told was very temperamental and tender—every now and then a trailing tendril gets knocked off so we tried potting them up. We have given several thriving little plants away and still have 5 at the moment!"—Blog post, marksvegplot.blogspot.com, Abi, 22 May 2017.

The 1812 Rose
Floribunda Rose
Rosaceae
Wilhelm Kordes & Söhne,
DE, 2007

Named to commemorate the War of 1812 in North America, which involved opposing British and United States armies, allied Indigenous Nations of Tecumseh's Confederacy, the Choctaw, Cherokee, Creek and Seneca Nations, and Spain, from the years 1812–1815.

The Heroes of Warsaw
Clematis/Waldrebe
Ranunculaceae
Szczepan Marczyński,
PL, 2019

Commemorates Polish civilian and military resistance to the German invasion of Warsaw in 1939.

Torpedo
Cuphea/Köcherblümchen
Lythraceae
breeder unknown

Tour de Malakoff
Centifolia Rose
Rosaceae
Pastoret, FR before 1856

Commemorates the French victory at Sevastopol, Crimean War, 1854—1855. The 'Tower of Malakoff' (tr. FR) formed part of the besieged city fortifications.

Trafalgar
Brussel Sprout/Rosenkohl
Brassicaceae
breeder and date unknown, GB

The Battle of Trafalgar, 1805, was a naval battle between Britian and France during the Napoleonic Wars (1799-1815). Naval Battle of Trafalgar, 1805, Napoleonic.

Unknown Warrior
Waterlily/Seerose
Nymphaeaceae
Marshall, date unknown

The grave of the Unknown Warrior in Westminster Abbey contains the remains of an unidentified British serviceman who was interred in 1920, symbolising the many killed service people who could not be repatriated from WWI battlefields.

Verdun
Polyantha Rose
Rosaceae
Barbier Frères & Co.,
FR, 1918

Named in commemoration of the 1916 Battle of Verdun, fought between French and German armies.

Victoire de la Marne
Peony/Pfingstrose
Paeoniaceae
Dessert & Méchin,
FR, 1915

The "Victory of the Marne" (tr. FR) refers to the French/Allied western front victory at the WWI Battle of the Marne.

Victoria Cross
Poppy/Mohnblume
Papaveraceae
breeder unknown

The Victoria cross is awarded for valour "in the presence of the enemy" to members of the British Armed Forces. The medals themselves are made from melted down cannons captured during previous British military engagements.

Warrior
Switchgrass/Rutenhirse
Poaceae
breeder unknown

Warzawska Nike
Clematis/Waldrebe
Ranunculaceae
Bruder Stefan Franczak,
Polish People's Republic, 1986

"Warsaw Victory" (tr. PL). Brother Stefan Franczak, a Polish clergyman and plant hybridiser, named many of his cultivar varieties after events in Polish military history, and Polish church figures. He dedicated this plant to the Polish resistance fighters of the 1944 Warsaw Uprising.

Water Soldier
Water Soldier/Stratiotes/Krebsschere
Hydrocharitaceae
breeder unknown

Common name is perhaps due to the sharpness of its serrated leaves.

Waterloo
Multiflora hybrid Rose
Rosaceae
Louis Lens, BE, 1989

The 1815 Battle of Waterloo.

Waterloo
Phlox/Flammenblumen
Polemoniaceae
breeder unknown

See above.

Westerplatte
Clematis/Waldrebe
Ranunculaceae
Bruder Stefan Franczak,
PL, before 1996

"Named to commemorate the heroes of the 1st armoured brigade of the Westerplatte peninsula at the Gdansk Bay. During the period between the First and the Second World War there was a Polish military unit at the border of Gdansk City. On the 1st September 1939 (4 a. m.) an

armoured German battleship 'Schleswig-Holstein' bombarded Westerplatte and this event marked the beginning of the Second World War. The Polish Westerplatte unit, numbering 182 soldiers, defended it against overwhelming Nazi forces for 7 days."
—Szczepan Marczyński, clematis hybridizer

White Admiral
Phlox/Flammenblumen
Polemoniaceae
Eugen Schleipfer,
Federal Republic of
Germany,1980

Winston Churchill
Sweet Pea/Duftwicke
Fabaceae
breeder unknown

Winston Churchill was the wartime Prime Minister of the UK from 1940—1945, and Prime Minister again from 1951—1955.

York and Lancaster
Rose
Rosaceae
First described by
Monardes, 1551

York and Lancaster were opposing houses of the 'War of the Roses', a civil conflict fought for control of the English thone. The conflict had its roots in the aftermath of the Hundred Year's War.

Zashchitnikam Bresta
Lilac/Flieder
Oleaceae
Bibikova & Smolskii,
UdSSR, 1964

"Heroes of Brest" (tr. RU). This lilac commemorates the defence of Brest fortress by Soviet troops in 1941 from Nazi German attack. Bred by scientific staff at the botanical garden of the Academy of Sciences in Minsk.

for an evolving list of Battlefield plant names, see website:
www.battlefield.garden

Dear Gabriella,   March 1st, 2024

I am writing this from Germany, to you in Australia. I am writing this during contested times, with a heavy heart. A few months back Australian voters rejected an alteration to the constitution to recognise and create a body for Indigenous Australians. Meanwhile, in Germany, a clandestine meeting of right-wing politicians, extremists and members of industries discuss a plan for a future expulsion of millions of people from Germany on the basis of racist criteria. And in the Middle East the Israeli army continues its offence in Gaza on a grand scale after the Oct 7 Hamas attack—spiking my own country's export of military gear and weapons.

Contested times are hardly new, if ever in doubt I could look at the long history of war and conflict as inscribed by each cultivar into the plant index of your installation Battlefield; and, of course, the further I expand the gaze from my desk outwards, the more pain and conflicts are bound to fall into focus. "In late 2022 I had planted 'Marine Corps' Daffodils," you wrote to me a few days ago, "their bulbs self-propagate, they split and multiply out of sight, underground. 2023 I was watching the soil, wondering how many there were hiding in the ground ready to sprout in spring, when rumours started on the radio about troops amassing at the Ukrainian-Russian border. Then Russia launched its invasion, and during that spring my sheltered understanding of war and peace, of buried violence, burst open." Like you, I cannot shake these events of on-going violence, of active—real and metaphoric—battlefields while writing a text on plants and politics for the Battlefield publication. I struggle to find words to describe my feelings, words that can hold meaning.

"Words are tricky and holding is complicated", Astrida Neimanis reminds me. "What are the words that can adequately hold the shared grief of these collapsing worlds?" I allow myself to be held by the words of others. "I write because I'm scared of writing but I'm more scared of not writing," explains Gloria Anzaldúa. I wish I had her bravery, to save—by the act of writing—myself, too, from the complacency she and I both fear.

I return to your work, Gabriella, to Battlefield, and I return to our friendship. I love Battlefield, in all its iterations so far: As a tiny yet wild gathering of plants in a community garden on Berlin's Tempelhofer Feld; as an ever-changing formation of military personnel structuring and re-structuring an exhibition space in Leipzig; as a large-scale garden design with historic references in the courtyard of a former cloister-turned-Kunsthalle in Osnabrück. And soon planted into the soil of the Augustaschacht memorial, a former Nazi forced labour site in Ohrbeck. I love the critical yet compassionate way of your thinking, present in the research for this project and throughout your overall practice. I love our friendship.

And I love that love—and care—for plants is as much part of this project as a history of political and military remembrance is. Love is a container for the plants and the artwork. In these times I realise that I need love to hold this text, too, or else risk writing from a place of grief. So let's begin with love as condition, as assignment, as provocation. Love for plants shall guide this text. But how to love a plant, then?

I remember the oldest record of a human-plant love story that I ever read. In Book XII of Pliny the Elder's Naturalis Historia (AD 77–79), I discovered a sequence that still touches my heart: "On a hill named Corne in the territory of Tusculum, near the city, there is a grove [...]. This grove contains one outstanding tree which in our generation excited the affection of the orator Passienus Crispus, who had twice been consul and who subsequently became still more distinguished by marrying Agrippina and becoming the stepfather of Nero; Crispus used regularly not merely to lie beneath the tree and pour wine over it, but to kiss and embrace it." Nero is still a child when his stepfather dies. In time, he will cut open the body of his mother whom he has sentenced to death; in time, he will see Rome burn for nine long days, destroying 10 of its 14 districts. I much prefer Crispus' quiet legacy of love to Nero's loud legacy of madness and pain. And, what's more, it is a legacy of interspecies, more-than-human love. He might, in fact, be one of the earliest dendrophiles on record. At his funeral, a rumour spread that Agrippina had poisoned her husband to gain his estate, but I wonder if she had murdered Crispus out of jealousy rather than greed. Not jealousy of the tree, per se, but jealousy of his ability to love and to care for another being—after all love has, as bell hooks attests to, a power to create transformative change.

But what is love anyway? Audre Lorde sees love as a force for empowerment, self-discovery, and connection: love is a complex and multifaceted force in our lives. Sara Ahmed describes love as entangled with power, politics, and social structures. For Ahmed, love's force manifests as orientation, as that which gives us a certain direction. Love can be liberating as well as constraining, it plays a role in shaping our lives and communities and is a powerful tool for solidarity and resistance against systems of oppression. Emphasising the importance of love as a practice of care and empathy can also be understood as a call to be less extractive. Less extractive and kinder. Before it is a feeling, bell hooks explains, love is an action with consequences.

If we speak about love, I feel, we should also mention consent: my friend Franca López Barbera introduced me to the Quebracho Colorado, a tree species growing in Northern Argentina. Local knowledge says that before approaching a Quebracho, one must greet him: "The salutation ["Buenos días, Senor Quebracho"] is not only an acknowledgement of his presence," she explains "but also a form of asking for permission to be physically close to him." To those it denies permission, the Quebracho will cause 'páaj', a rash that can be cured by apologising and offering a sign of friendship to the tree. Acknowledging a tree's capacity for consent means centring the tree politically as capable of decision-making. And by understanding it as a relational being, the tree—and Nature—seizes to be a mere resource. While Quebrachos don't grow in Tusculum, I still like to think that the love story between Crispus and his tree was a consensual one, too. He practically wined and dined it, after all.

You have spoken about how Battlefield is, to you, a process of gardening history, of tending to written time. These plants, absurdly tied through nomination to historical actions, living memory of which they may long outlive and overgrow, as a means to understand the leakiness of history. In my notes I see that exactly a year ago, on February 16, 2023, I started researching komatiites, a type of ultramafic mantle-derived volcanic rock gone extinct. I am still baffled by the idiosyncrasy of a stone that is here—though rare—and simultaneously extinct, given that the conditions necessary for its emergence have irrevocably passed. Komatiite's existence in different realities disrupts the linearity of time as we narrate it. Another character challenging the life-death binary is so-called zombie moss: a moss specimen dug up in 2014 from an island in Antarctica where it had been buried in permafrost for 1500 years, now rising again and regenerating new plants in the scientific laboratory of researchers from the British Antarctic Survey and Reading University. Both zombie moss and komatiite are bridges to an in-between space, navigating the pathways between the living and the dead. Both, stone and moss, are coexisting and unravelling in their own respective time; they are a material of living memory, of living and grieving.

Gloria Anzaldúa introduces me to the concept of 'Nepantla', the threshold, the in-between space. Nepantla, a Nahuatl word, signifies the liminal space where love often resides for marginalised individuals who navigate multiple worlds: "Transformations occur in this in-between space, an unstable, unpredictable, precarious, always-in-transition space lacking clear boundaries. Nepantla es tierra desconocida, and living in this liminal zone means being in a constant state of displacement—an uncomfortable, even alarming feeling. [...] Though this state links us to other ideas, people, and worlds, we feel threatened by these new connections and the change they engender." There are, of course, challenges and possibilities of love in these liminal spaces, as well as acceptance and cultural affirmation—and in this space, she would argue, self-love is of great importance. Anzaldúa teaches me how mourning can be a form of resistance and a way to honour marginalised histories and identities.

I take long breaks in between writing this text, stuck in my very own nepantla-like state of living and grieving. Words seem too heavy and at the same time not meaningful enough. Words seem stretched to their limit. "Language, like living, also always fails", Neimanis reminds me.

On my laptop I store a document which contains a random collection of moments when botanical descriptions, metaphors and symbolism are used in political speech. The latest entry is from December 8, 2023. It is a quote by Robert Wood, the US deputy ambassador who vetoed the UN resolution calling for a ceasefire in Gaza: "[...] we do not support calls for an immediate ceasefire. This would only plant the seeds for the next war...". But, I would argue, botanically speaking, the seeds we plant are seeds of love. Lately I have been thinking a lot about seeds, about seed banks, seed scarcity. Seeds are treasured, kept in vaults and banks, handled with knowledge and care, watered and watched over with affection, their growth anxiously awaited with a hopeful heart. You don't plant seeds of hate, you plant what you long for to return—to bloom!—in the future. You don't plant out of hate but hope—though you might try to bury what you hate or fear.

"The soil has a shocking and satisfying secret life that will only be revealed to you in increments," whispers Mika Conradie. "We give lip service to acceptance, as though acceptance were enough," joins Octavia E. Butler. "What didn't you do to bury me / but you forgot that I was a seed," repeats Dinos Christianopoulos.

I think about Battlefield and I wonder if eventually there will be a plant cultivar remembering the current conflict in Gaza. But what are the chances that this future plant will be called 'Ceasefire' and not 'Iron Sting', or 'Dumb Bomb' or after any other of the weapons systems employed against civilians there? And when will we see its bloom? Afterall, Reimer Kordes introduced his 'Atombombe' rose not even ten years after the horrific atomic bombings of Hiroshima and Nagasaki.

Another poem by Christianopoulos comes to my mind; one that talks about love, describing love as "[...] above all a verification of our loneliness, when we try to perch on a hard-to-conquer body." What if this hard to conquer body is solidarity, is empathy? I wanted to hold on to love so that I would not slip into grief. I remember Billy-Ray Belcourt describing love as a process of becoming unbodied, so maybe love is not the absence of grief. Grief is what stays when love no longer has a body. Grief is like phantom limb pain, a feeling with no body to hold it. What aches us, after we fall apart is the phantom limb of empathy, the phantom limb of humanity. Grief work, I understand, is paying attention to the losses a body cannot incorporate. And just as with love, Ahmed and Lorde would probably tell me, grief, too, needs to be reflected within broader cultural contexts. Grief too, I understand, is intertwined with power, identity and social structures.

I allow myself, one more time, to be held by the words of others. A few days ago I read Poem Number Two on Bell's Theorem, or The New Physicality of Long Distance Love (1994) by June Jordan, and its words still resonate in my head:

> There is no chance that we will fall apart
> There is no chance
> There are no parts.

In this time of contention I cannot think of a better invocation for and of love to end this with.

With love,
Anja

P.S. I am thankful for the poetry, films and texts by Sara Ahmed, Gloria Anzaldúa, Emilia Beatriz, Billy-Ray Belcourt, Octavia E. Butler, Dinos Christianopoulos, Mika Conradie, Meghan Hayes, bell hooks, June Jordan, Franca López Barbera, Audre Lorde, Astrida Neimanis, and Deborah Stratman. Their words and thoughts hold and inspire me.